Darkest December

Darkest December

Chiara Evans

Dedicated to my Father, Robert S. Evans
And my good friend, Adam A. Olalde

Dear Dad I

And it breaks my very soul to see your
smile
Just because I carry it well doesn't mean it
doesn't hurt

Intuition

We were never introduced
I simply knew you
All of you and all at once
There were no secrets between us
You were everything you
Showed yourself to be
We never had to get to know one another
We learned each other through growth

The Knot, Part I

Coming across the knot,
It can be intriguing to try and untie,
Come on,
Try your hand!
Can you solve the puzzle of the knot?
Its intricacies wound up tight
Underlying patterns fascinating to the sight
A mess of rope
Existing in infinite space
Piece by piece
Added ever so carefully
Tied with love, hate, fear, and longing
What's on the surface
Appears beautiful, opalescent
Still, it is screaming underneath
The hidden complexities
Bursting below
Suffocating certain patterns
So pluck away
Some ends were better left to fray
Tied into a colorful abstract
Connected and lost within themselves
The knot goes forever on and on
Easily solved at the beginning

Harder to relieve later
Do you think you can untie the knot?
What if you get it fully undone?
What once existed
A masterpiece of experience
Will be forever lost
And at what cost?
Ends cut most frequently
A strange unseen force of organization
Working against the layers of time
Solving the puzzle of the knot
Who knows if it will prevail?

Nocturnal Strangers

There's a silent urgency in this deafening emergency

We're pleading, we're bleeding, but still, mind over matter sweetie

It isn't easy but it's here

This duality serves neither of us, but still we're painting faces with fresh blood

We see lurkers, hiding within the trees and skittering between shadows

The darkness wraps around us all, both sword and shield

Still every night plays out the same

And the morning will never touch us, at least not unless we want it to

Just remember though not this time, there's a lot of bad, and beware

Within Smoke

The candle burns bright
beside the fire tonight
And there's another glow emanating from
the tip of your lips
The walls are dancing amongst the lights
Smoke circles trilling a storied yellow halo
above your head
The heavens in your mind begin to part

You're sitting with your hands
grasping the chair arms
Head up and clouds spewing from your
mouth, creating sky
Universes enter and stars are in your eyes
All thoughts are jumping, crashing,
evolving into more
The pit within tears you apart

Yet we are married to the bliss of
escaping the inescapable
You and I wish to defeat that harsh reality
pounding upon us
Fogging our judgment and hiding
within smoke

From the darkness comes light and
from hell there is heaven
Pain gives pleasure a new start

Lounge Song

The lights are way down low
All the room seems to stop
and swirl in smoke
I've written a beautiful melody
You helped to write the words
Just give me a moment to prove
If only you'd let my heart call out true
It's a message
I've been trying to get through
My voice will be so sweet, ever so elegant,
soft and harmonious
Let me sing you a song
The one that I should have all along
I put it off for too much time
Now the curtain is closing
The bartender says it's last call
But I'm still singing
The harmony joins and the players play
Let me please sing for you
The way I was meant to
My darling we're the same shade of blue
And without you this has no meaning
The energy is fleeting
You were the beat, the tune, the key

You can try to close the curtain on me
Turn out the lights, shut off the stage
I will keep singing
With the words in my soul
This thing was real
Just could never come together
Always out of time
Let me sing you a song
The words now never felt so strong
You've been saying I was wrong
To feel this rhythm
To put words to a page
I wish I could sing for you
But the notes all flicker and disappear
My voice begins to give out
Just as you told me there was nothing left
Give me a chance
Let me start again and sing you a song
The one that I should have all along
The one with meaning
That only you can divine
Go ahead and walk out
I'll still be singing this song for you

Matrices

Are we forever questioning?
With leaves in our hair and
droplets on our faces
Our fates have intertwined in
infinite entanglements
Growing exponentially
While others disintegrate
The strands cross as we touch, as we love
Our webs grow wider the more you are near
We move forward and out of the past
Storms are heaving
The clouds stretching, parting
And their silence mocks us without a word
For we will never comprehend why we meet
Who affects us and how
But nature is deafening
In its beautiful complexity
We are but passengers in the world
Traveling along paths we make
Until it's the end of our sweet universe

Dear Dad II

Cold: That's my last memory of you
How fucking horrible

Staring Contests

I learned you the hard way,
and the right way the first time
In the back of my mind, I've often told you
I've always been more sadness,
Not actually someone
If I were to get better then,
Where would you go?
I know what healing means for you and me
It means cuts and scars,
washing away blood
Stitches, glue, and explanations
for the wounds
Tears and invitations for disaster
No more arm-wrestling matches
or staring contests
But mostly it's saying things
Things I can't take back
That's not something I am strong enough
to survive
Because losing you could be
worse than living with you

Anima Bella

One eye was red and the other was white
She caught herself searching in the dead
of the night
Looking for all the time
she couldn't replace
She wondered how she could ever be
the optimist
But she kept walking

She's being broken down to fragments,
piece by piece
Torn into by the thoughts that never seem
to cease
She stepped with purpose, lightly and fluid
Gathering sparks at her fingers and smoke
on her lips
As she kept walking

Against the rocks, arrows, and all else they
could throw
Her scars were melting away,
little did they know
The heat was growing, frequency ringing
Little else could anyone do to stop her

And she kept walking

Soon beginning behind her the colors
would change
The shimmering haze and world above
soon became strange
Teeth echoed without sound and
reverberated in this battlefield
The dissonant piano chords
fading off in the distance
Then she kept walking

She had dark smears on her face
Ashen warrior paint as a saving grace
She stepped with steel and out of the clouds
Emerging brighter, catching fire
Still, she kept walking

Contortion

I stretch and twist
Trying to fit into place
I contort my body into each shape
The one you want to see
But I know it isn't real, isn't me
The funhouse mirror images viewed
Err on the side of caution
Around the box you placed me in
I will not be contained
I curve and elongate to match and mimic
For along the edges nothing enwraps
Adaptation in the true intelligence
and God's design but
I'm the puzzle piece that
doesn't fit into the bigger picture

You Only Ever Get Glimpses, Fractions

I don't understand why I keep
catching you looking me over
I don't know what it is you see
But perhaps it is quite different than
that what is truly me
Perhaps it is not what I think you see
But I know for sure it is not reality

I try to ignore it when you're
looking me up and down
But there's a revolt in my head
All the different versions of me
I must amend
Are constantly at a divide, cannot be
put to bed
For they are part of infinity, you said
A universe within my head

I don't know if these mirrors make me
more sober or more drunk
I guess I'll never know what you truly think
There's no way to swim in infinity,
I only ever sink
Which one is real, which one will last?

All these thoughts can drive one
to the brink
I don't know for sure my reality, but I'm
trying to get all in sync
And I'm not scared of you anymore

This Must Be A Hoax

It feels darker still
Somehow the sun is shining
And everything keeps on going
But the world stops and looks
It takes a glance
Judges briefly, wonders a moment
Whilst moving away at a pace
Only some know how to follow
And your hands outstretched
You're asking why
But they've already gone
Hair billowing in the wind
and shoes clicking
You'll not get your answer
How do I walk on?
Where do you go when
everything starts coming undone?
All of my time spent waiting by the phone
For a call or text that never came
You never even really noticed me
Yet I am, and always will be,
The one to blame
Just further down the line,
Further in the coals, the flame

And you, you could learn a thing or two
If you only paid attention

Methuselah

I did not think when I threw myself
over the edge
That I would be born again at the bottom
Come back to life with arms outstretched
Darling, I do that all the time
It's no enemy next to my passivity
In a fair fight I would've won
I put up no shield
To the hateful tongues and hands
I even wished them well
As they ran me through
Then the prying eyes watched me
fall to my knees
Remove the sword while I was bleeding out

I did not think when I blocked my lungs
That I would breathe ever again
Honey, dying's the easy part
I am no executioner, I am the prisoner
Of little consequence though
For some reason God is on my side
I still believe
Though there's myriad cracks He can see
And I thanked Him when

All I've loved was destroyed
Do not ask the price I've paid
I must live with
these consequences I've weighed

I did not think when I died it would
be the first time
That my eyes would see the light
and open again
Dear, at first I fought with my time
Now I long to grow old, I felt the
switch in my head
No, I will not speak of any of my sins
And the flaws and weakness of my heart
The burdens I carry for this conservation
Wasn't it Him, who said
I needed to change?
That's when I used to be
Off route and out of time
I will survive alone, when He kills me,
over and over
Because
He can take from my eyes, the pain entire
And that is what I truly desire

Dear Dad III

The Spanish language treats
dying and death as temporary
Which I once thought was beautiful,
but it's just naïve

What Makes Up the Soul

If the body is a reflection of the soul
Mine would be battered and scarred
Constantly aching, hurting
It's dull but healing throughout the eons
Mine is in pain, anxious, sad, always alert
If the eyes are windows to the soul
Mine would be tearful and red
Deep with love, but bloodshot and tired
I take light in and try to shine myself
Waiting and wishing to see that
part of me again
My soul longs for you
This is mirrored in my pain
My soul, it struggles to shine these days
Yet here comes a glow up
through the cracks
If the soul is what determines beauty
How will mine ever be made whole?
It's green with envy and full of spite
Angry at things for having not gone right
It will need a good polish and a reassurance
That it will be okay
And if the soul is weighed when we get to
Heaven

If I ever get to heaven for the nights like this
Mine sure is heavy
Pulled down by the weight of all the years
From facing my demons through
so many tears
My soul is broken
How will I ever be okay again?
If you're not here to tell me I will be?

The Time Has Come

I'm at my strongest when I'm under attack
So come at me; come get me
You won't like how I fight back
I see beauty in what you cannot see

I'm most decisive when I'm challenged
So hate me; you aren't me
You didn't like how you scavenged
My leftover scraps of personality

Don't you dare tell me that I'm nothing
You're no match for me
I can't believe this is all over one thing
I am more than you and I am free

Privilege

I never got to eat all of my Halloween candy
I had to pick it all apart, go back and restart
And remove just about half each year so my
Dad could eat it instead
Now that's no one's fault and I'm not mad
but
I bet you don't know
what that feels like

I moved around a bunch
when I was younger
Maybe that's why things never felt
really quite stable
Had to keep packing it up and go where
we were able
Whatever we could afford and just the
three of us
Now in that situation I knew exactly
who to blame and
I bet you don't really know
what that feels like

I didn't have a lot of toys and
so I made my own

I didn't like to share because then people
would know
How little we had and that I didn't
want to show
I just remember being embarrassed and
wanting to go
I guess that doesn't really matter much but
There was so much I missed out on and
I bet you don't know what that feels like

I only got to see my Dad infrequently
for a short amount of time
He'd smile and get us dinner
He would say he loves us and it's fine
But I knew something wasn't right
Even at such a young age because
I remembered
What things were like before and
I bet you don't know what that feels like

I watch and I long for the new places
Everywhere you were able to go and
the new skies
My goodness this is when I found out
how time flies
The bustling cities, sandy beaches, sunrises,

hikes, and beauty you get to see
Well guess what I bet you can tell
that was never me
I'm always left behind, never to escape
I know you don't know what that feels like

I knew something was missing and
something was wrong
They always had some criticism or
something about which to complain
I never really knew why
she could never look into my eyes,
through tears and see all the pain
I never wanted this name
Everything was about her at the hospital
and that made me feel like
I was going insane
And you just simply don't know
what that feels like
All of these things that you might take
for granted
I wish you'd show some gratitude
Because there are a lot of things that
you get to have and do
Yet for me it will never be true
There isn't a next time

You don't know what that feels like

You don't know everything
another goes through
I'm not trying to play the victim and
I don't want your sympathy
Just don't judge the very little that you see
Because you have that privilege
You got a lot of things I wish I
could have had and now I never can
And
I bet
You don't know
What that feels like

Rage

I got my hopes up
And smashed them to pieces
Disemboweling them
with my own weapons
Slashing their blood on my
cheeks and corneas
My own scars still haven't healed
From where they fought back

This will always be dangerous
I won't let you see it, but
It's in the eyes, the heartless one
I look back grinning
With my hands at their throats
The betrayal of my dreams is palpable

Perhaps my sympathies lie with them
But it's easier to sacrifice them now
Letting the light diminish while
Clawing at my grip, beating me
It's not until they've faded away
And the world is in black and white

I see what I've done, I've come to
I dropped the stained dagger
and my fists fell
In my fevered frenzy,
This attempt at protection
My lies, I thought they loved me
That's why I did it
I just don't remember

Resistance

With this newfound remedy
My words have lost all meaning
What there once was
Has left me
Oh muse
Why have you forsaken me?
I didn't know I would have
To sacrifice one for the other
An impossible choice
Oh muse
Won't you come back to me?

Foreign Land

I didn't realize how far behind we were
My words fell on deaf and dumb ears so
I gave all my trust,
my heart to those above
At the top of this hill and
hoped for the best
Knowing all of this I'm sure to return
home and never rest
Now I beg you to collect your papers
and reasons alike
Pray you never have this same
kind of plight
You should regret that you didn't
know me at first
I am the eldest one
You might just move on without
looking back
But you need to face what you've done
And do your time

Do you remember how it was
at the start?
You made it seem less of a science and
more of an art

If it hadn't been kept secret I never
would have agreed
You spent too much time going
back and forth
Hemming and hawing so much
I had to come back up north
The land never felt so cold and
unforgiving
It seemed so hostile and yet it's
something I keep on reliving
I cannot forgive these mistakes
I am the eldest one
I stood at the edge of the tarmac and
took a deep breath
Letting myself contemplate
the run up to death
You imbeciles know not what is in store

I am your priority now sir, listen to me!
You never answered my question and
couldn't even bother to see!
How are you okay with those events
and what you do?
Your failures reek and so do you
The days went by quiet and unchanged

My fingers tapping impatiently,
it's all so strange
The days grew long and there was
no one at home, no one at work
Even though we knew, the dread kept
building
You should've seen me before
I am the eldest one
Seems you gave up and did nothing,
which I can prove
But doing something, anything
should have been your move

The next I come back to that now
hard and foreign land
I will take a deep breath, yes just the one
I will go down the hall and
pick up my gun
You'll think I'm familiar, but
you can't remember why
Well, I am the eldest one
That will be the day when I finally
catch your eye
And you'll have to plead to the
gods you've always defied
You'll be forced to look back

at my empty lips
For I don't think I can add any
postscripts
You've no legs to stand and no escape
Because you had no right to take that soul
Which was supposed to be mine

Wrath

This heart, it's only human
But the devil got me
Instilled in it an anger
Created long ago
One that ever only came
And went in another form
It learned to hide
With the guise of melancholy
It's beginning to wear off now
And the true purpose
Of all this suffering
Is beginning to ring
Tolling for thee
It lives, this gift
In the spaces
Between facts and fictions
Where no one would ever think to look
A lonely, tired girl
A daughter of strife
One with a long memory
An everlasting patience
An anger soon to be feared
And a sense of justice to be venerated

The mutterings of despair
Have been quietly filled with rage
Behind closed doors
Can't you see these demons inside?
They're rearing to run
Can't hold them for long
A shadow of the former self remains
The path to heaven
Runs straight through
The evasive depths of hell
This heart is not the same as it once was
The walls are crumbling down
The transformation taking hold
I always knew
What I'd do to you
If I ever
Found your dreams

Dear Dad IV

I'm afraid to go outside today
Because the world doesn't care you're gone
anymore

I Am From

I am from pencils
From Dell and Ticonderoga
And where the pencil meets the page
The space between light and shadow
Where substance meets imagination
I am from challenges
Being told I'm not good enough
Pressing through to create what I believe
And from blossoms on the tree
I am from the effort
Coaches made me give
Never allowed to give up
From purple and orange painted skies
Glowing with residual light
I am from courtesy
Leaving them alone when it's all bad
And kicking the dead horse
Though I try not to
From caring for the little things
And remembering all I've been through
I am from yells of disapproval
And the occasional half-meant 'good job'
From 'the world's all good'
To the mess they all made

A land left forsaken and to live upon
its own
Building rebuilding
I am from across the sea
With lovely sundries and patience there
From the skylines of cities on the water
Reaching towards the clouds
From people who act like they care
And then turn their backs to others
To hurt them while silent, hypocrites
I am from worlds
I view upon the screen
From the words upon pages
The cry of 'I have become death,
destroyer of worlds'
I am from persistence
Because I will get through the storm
I am from pencils
Where the tip meets the page
The space between heard and unheard
Where I create and build

What If

What if I had gotten it right?
Then you'd still be here by my side
Then I'd still have someone to walk with
What if there was light in your darkness?
What if I had cut back your restraints?
And taken the poison off the shelf?
What if you had been yourself?
And what if now with the danger here,
You could be standing without fear?
Oh I'd give anything to hold your hand
Not to have felt the ice within and
To give you something better than I had
Every step forward I take away from you
Oh it's the hardest thing I'll ever do
I didn't want to fail you but it's true
And myself and the day were all so blue
What if I had been better?
Focused on the real things that matter?
Reached out harder and faster?
What if you were afraid?
What if I had been there with you
at the fall?
Oh for the love of God I'd give it all

Ginger Cat, Tabby Cat

After each of my worst life periods
I got a cat
A soft comfort for a sharp world
One with love that I could raise
Something I could protect
I needed something good
Something pure
I take out the time to help them grow
A reminder of where I've been
And what I have gone through
That I made it out alive
When others did not
That I was successful
When I was at my lowest
After each time I was at the bottom
And had gone further down than before
I got a cat
They mark the hardships
They mark my acceptance
Of the difficulty in the world
And they make me happy
When everything is painful
They are a piece of love
A reminder that it will be all right

I will not let you go gently into the
good night

Lag

Imagine this is black and white
Garbled speech and smiles
I have lost nine minutes of my time
Stolen from me by an unknown force
I don't know if I feel alive
I listen to the same sad songs over and over
This is my religion
Imagine this in technicolor
Rumbling noise and faces with masks
I keep losing my time
I try not to overthink it

Transforming

I am the empty space left untended
Even stars flicker
Light will dim sometimes
Bursts of flame come flying free recklessly
On some nights some fires look brighter
Even stars burn out
Even stars die

I am the trees in winter
Appearing dead yet still alive
Deep within me something is stirring
Whilst my leaves have fallen
A blanket on the forest floor to
keep me warm
I withstand the hellish landscape
Frozen over
Standing tall still with heaps of snow
Buckling my branches
Don't know when it will go

I am the cocoon and closed inside
Maybe one day soon I can paint the skies
With cirrus clouds and deep purples

Aquas and royal blues with
dots of cumulus
I would make them in your image
That could be your legacy

The Broken Heart

Two squares and one circle
As your heart beats and
Your lungs fill with air
Tiled grids and white walls
No news
Two squares, one circle
Counting the seconds you are away
I breathe in
My heart skips a beat
Tears well up
I breathe out
I feel the love
The worry
The regret
The bodies leaning against the wall
A hand to the paint and head bowed
Two squares, one circle
We can't speak
Eleven petals
One flower at the center of it all
My hands into fists they ball
Frustration and anxiety
The pain of hopelessness
Powerlessness

Loneliness
Tightness
Electric crackling in and out of time
Pressure building on my mind
Two squares, one circle
It's happening again
I can't breathe
Sympathetic suffocation
I refuse all oxygen
Because it's happening again
And I won't leave you again
I'm sorry I did

Dear Dad V

Giving your eulogy was the hardest thing
I have ever had to do
It is the hardest thing I will ever do

The Beast that Lies Below

The beast that lies below
It has a hold around my throat
Why I can never make it let go
Its claws are sharp, and any
sudden movement might do the trick
I wish you could understand
How I must beware the nails that are dirty
and stained with opium
I know everyone feels sad sometimes
Or has a bad day
I know I shouldn't take it out on others
That is not fair
But I have bad days most days
It's always hanging on
It's a very rare occurrence when
happiness creeps in
I wish you could understand
In my reasoning, logic tells me
I don't have it that bad
Others' homes are at war and others have
Entire tides to fight against
Others have poison raining from the sky
and still others are trapped
That doesn't mean I can stop feeling

The way I do
Sometimes there's not a choice
I wish you could understand
The chemicals in my brain simply
won't work that way
They barely make it across the synapse
Before they are snatched away
The scaffolding I take to save them
Doesn't always work
Doesn't always make me feel better
It is not the cure all, be all that
YOU want it to be
I wish you could understand
I don't exist to be what you want me to be
I don't choose to be unbalanced
The width of the beam changes day to day
And my grip is weaker than
the beast's some moments
As above, so it is below

Self-Immolation

It's keeping me warm
Singeing my edges slowly
These rewritten drafts,
Their pages curling inward
This pain became
Gasoline
I didn't think you'd ever be
The flint to strike
And destroy me
The blaze is out
But even still
Embers burn just the same
Grief is a fire
Ever burning
Because without you
I feel
I am without myself

Fragmented

Perfectly imperfect
Yet she can do all of this
Won't she listen to the universe
It's so sad to think about the pain
But it's so good to see
All of these layers blooming back
For all of her problems
For all of her ribbons holding her back
She will pull through,
Her chest heaving forward
She knows there's no place for emotion
On the battlefield
But she won't forget the memories
What made her who she is
For all of the pain
She creates love
Yet she doesn't heed her orders
She's struggling to break free
These ideas are chains
They are forged of steel and
speaking in tongues
The voices inside are drawing her back
again
From all of her time in cruelty and war

She still has shrapnel buried underneath
Slowly it is cutting her free
Everything holding her back
She's fighting with her weak hand
Standing before conquerors
Doing their best
To do what they do best
Holding the weight of it
All on her shoulders
Still she could do all of this
She plucked dreams from the sky
And made them reality with ease
Yet I cannot remember who she really was

The 4th

It's 23:18
And creeping closer to your last day
I sit petrified
Regretting what I didn't know
The loss of memories
Yet to be made
Things that should have been
Would have been
But it was stolen away
The things which could have been
This is what aches
Every day lately it's all I feel

Have I Experienced This Before?

I thought you were supposed to wake from
nightmares
Seems I keep walking through them
Dark shadows as my companions
Used to be just one
More continually gathering now
A pack of wild dogs
Without discipline they consume
Everything I have
I thought dreams were supposed
to come true
I didn't think that included night terrors
Does it make sense to feel anymore?
I keep waiting for everything to end
I didn't know that was also
under the umbrella
I thought I went past that long ago

Milestones

That silent storm does brew
On the horizon and all at once
The quartz and glistening waves are
harbingers
Of greater sound and fury still
Questions
Of the natural order and studies of ologies
Perhaps not a match for the
Forthcoming end to silence
The fractures found in the most
Beautiful of crystals are dreams
spinning out of place
This most perfect juxtaposition of
looking for the footsteps left behind
And the unraveling of expectations
These lumps of coal dare
never to be diamonds
For the lack of pressure keeps them so
The storm sweeping closer
Bringing me the horizon with
Bowed head and upon bended knee
A hollow crown it is yet bears weight of
all anticlimax and the ineffable
Adorned with precious stones

Each a different shade and hue
Colors of beauty and meaning
Yet dull within the rays of light which
Shine for thee
The foam, it spits and with dull teeth
it bites
Encouraged by the wind as it strengthens
The line between the heavens and
Earth is finally erased but only a moment
And here they touch as a flicker, hesitantly
Lightening scattering out into the sea
Now one can say the storm has broken its
vow

Resurgence

I'm drowning in red blood
I can feel the wounds all over me
They're resurfacing
Fresh blood
These scars are waking up again
These enemies are staring at me
My fears are taking hold
I'm swimming in dark blood
My emotions are at the brim
Spilling over
And I'm swimming in this endless sea
Fresh blood over my face
I won't let this all be for nothing
Even though I'm outnumbered
I'll keep my head above
All that's left of myself
Are the gaps in what little self-confidence
I still have
I will let myself drown
Only so I can rise back up again
And hope I can catch my breath

Bereaved

I want to know
Where I should go
Home to feel safe again
I want to know
When I can
Start feeling myself again
I'm a stranger to myself
But for once
My head and my heart
Feel the same

Just Above The Surface

All of a sudden there arises
A slab of concrete sidewalk
I can't dive deep into the pool and dance
Around down there
All I can do is walk on air
While stuck just above the surface

The water is comforting,
warm to the touch
Above the surface is windy, unfamiliar
I look longingly down into the depths
See shapes undulating and the footpaths
I used to take
I test each new piece, fearing it is fake
Making my way just above the surface

My fingers write sonnets in ripples
But cannot penetrate further
My words are carried away instantly
by the gusts
From this realm I can see my old world
I try to grasp at shades escaping from
my fingers curled
I am the only above the surface

The days rattle on without ceremony
The sidewalk tracks tesselate and breathe
I recognize little still, all is strange
Even if I try to fall back into the sea
My limbs are motionless for they disagree
So I stop fighting, stop fixating on where
I used to exist
Keeping my peripheral vision
Just above the surface

Through the quicksilver clouds,
The light is cutting
The wind dies down and the surface
becomes glass
The boundary becomes more solid,
the ocean is more shallow
I never knew what I was making,
or that I was creating
I thought I was disconnected, not waiting
Terraforming this world above the surface

Dear Dad VI

I made a promise that now I can't keep
I guess it's okay, but it's my last thought
before I fall asleep

The Knot, Part II

Here lay these pieces of rope and string
Once part of a palpable dream
Now they may be damaged,
But they are not forgotten
Collect them up
Tie them tight
Use all your might
They come together, they are meant to be
Weave them in and out
Around and within themselves
With them build a monument
Healed, and shining
Keep it growing
Protect the core
So that each strand may find the light
It is worth the battle
The pain, sweat, tears, and blood
To make a knot most stunningly sanguine
Out of the leaden past
All its obscurities will never be known
All this makes a knot most sleek and strong
One that cannot be cut by
Even the sharpest of swords
One that will bear the weight of the world

At both ends
This purposeful tangle will not unravel
And will never fray and with each new layer
The score of all the years is kept
All of time is known
It is with this
You anchor yourself on the climb to
Heaven
Though leagues of fiery Hell
Protect your sanity
These trials enforce the knot
None will pick its end
That which is built upon truth and love
Few will learn to create it
Even fewer will add to its broken beauty
Allow it to grow
Learn its pattern
Both fast and slow
It will fasten you
Remember
All this from those imperfect pieces
Whoever thought this could be
A knot like this is a sight to behold
Use it and know this knot will hold

Resilience and Desperation

We were held from the skyline
Dizzily straining to get down
But their fingers and thumbs were
too strong
The puddles of pavement and
The splashes of steel
That's what scared you the most
What made you fall
You were the only, you were the one
The one that was tired of the setting sun
Darkness impedes on hope
This was a long and weary wait
To get away from the crowd of jagged teeth
Ready to pierce us when the hands let go
I won't bury you in honor
Because if you die I won't be here
Still I wrenched myself from
their pressurized grasp
Tore you from their clutches and
Made you part of my world
Now, Life and Death,
They can never touch you
I'm not going to be the soldier
That the General sends in alone, unarmed

You put faith in me that I would
Get you back to safety
Think about what I just said
No matter what you do
I'll catch you if all you do is fall
And I will speak to you even if
You won't speak at all

Apocalypse

Why do the birds keep on singing?
Why does the wind swirl around?
They should know better
Than to allow the world to turn
My heart stopped when you turned away
The clouds came overhead and I
I began to cry
But not for long because I knew
This was the end of the world
The end of all that had been
And I wanted to see
But why does the sun keep shining?
And how can the flowers blossom
and leaves unfurl?
They all know now
The Earth has been shattered
Yet they keep on
My mind went numb for a time and I
I refused to lay down and die
Because even though
It's the end of today
The world will still be there tomorrow
And I
I will survive the end of the world

The Constant Reminders

Hands made rough from hard work
Cuts you couldn't feel,
Calluses that protected you from harm
The orange haze made
by the red and yellow stoplights
Bits of fluff and fuzz
from the German shepherds
Stacks of photos, slides, and film
Baseball hats soaked with sweat
Tools strewn over your workbench
Loose nails, screws, washers, bits and bobs
Carefully organized bins of memories and
Things you might need
Leopard print and silver cars
A wispy, clouded night with a full moon
That green foam you use with fake flowers
Gardening soil and rehoming new plants
The bee pinned to the wall
Red rubber covered stairs with circles
So you don't slip
Warm toasted bagels and
blueberry pancakes
Made perfectly round and perfectly cooked

Cholesterol content and agave
Curved and bubbled handwriting,
done with care
Poking and pecking at keyboard keys
Talk to text and surprisingly emojis
Airplanes and jets flying overhead,
the contrails
A fluffy blanket and another of
grey and black patterns
Your college t-shirts preserved oh so well
The doorframe
The one where our heights were marked
The soft smell of darkroom chemicals
The itch I can never scratch
Red and brown beards and
Glasses without frames
Messy baseboards and window frames
Ones with paint marks
Times I almost get run over
While crossing the busy streets
Once in a while,
When I say something you used to
Sitting alone in the doctor's waiting room
Reaching over open cans and jars
Classical music and NPR
Snowblowers and clean driveways

Everything that is always neat
These are just some of the things
that turn my thoughts to you

Damaged

If I broke you down into fragments and
If I put you back together piece by piece
Would you still be as beautiful?

Itch

Sometimes there's a slight itch
And I have the compulsion to scratch
But I remember it's tender there,
I remember
How it got there
I know more eyes than mine have seen it
And people have probably noted it
But I choose to ignore the itch most days
I wish it weren't there
Sometimes I feel
It gets tighter
Almost suffocating, blinding
All my thoughts turn to the feeling
Of skin and flesh rippling open and
Bones shattering under the surface
Sometimes
Sometimes I keep it hidden
Hiding it in hopes others won't see it
It's a constant reminder
Of the battle raging on
Sword versus sword
Steel reverberating against steel
If you have the same tools,
Then it's just a question of skill

But I'm fighting with my weak hand
Sometimes it itches
And I'm reminded of you
Telling me it will fade over time
It won't be this red and dark forever
You took my hands in yours
And when I think of that
It doesn't itch anymore

As for Me, I Waited,
Longer than is Clear

I thought I'd gotten over it, I wasn't lost
Turns out the feeling wasn't over and
I started going back there
Since nothing has changed me quite like
Those days, but still
There's nothing I wouldn't do to pay off
my debts in Heaven
I know I've been a stranger lately;
I can't make out any of these passing faces
I've been caught in the throes of waves
And serotonin syndroming
I've been stuck staring at the ragged skyline
And shouting from the rooftops
Blowing through the days without
direction
Since you took me to the top and let me fall
I know I ran away and I let you down
There's nothing I wouldn't do to
escape these feelings
Some day I'm going to make it right
Other days when I fall to my knees
I'm thinking there's nothing left

And yet it's such a mystery I don't
understand
I still get back up for you, only because of
you
I think pain is
Waiting alone by the window, forcing it
Trying to help you get back home soon
It was looking like everything was fine
I don't think I'll ever be able to move on
But I know there's only one life for sure and
I want to be free from the bad dreams

Reconstruction

And after the wreck
The mile markers all look the same
The numbers all blur into one
I don't know how far I've gone
And how much more there is go
To get away from all the debris
I just keep looking back at the mangled steel
Yeah, I'm still alone out here
I should be the one dead

The other driver must have seen me
Yet managed still to hit me with inelasticity
Dragged my car for what seemed an age
Spinning me around and upside down
But I got out, I needed help
But no one else was there, just us
I walked away reluctantly and, in a daze
Yeah, my injuries will never heal completely
I can't help but keep picking at them

When I blink the reality disappears for a
moment
I stagger forward and away
My breath and body shaking, mind and

marrow bleeding
The crash, and the pain, just salt in the
wound
I can't help but wonder why and what to
do next
Did they do it on purpose or was it an
accident?
No one could fix this, the damage is done
Nothing will ever be the same
As it was before
Maybe that was the point?

Dear Dad VII

Sometimes it gives me comfort
That we believed, and looked at it the same

The Voices

Out of the depths
Through the dirt and the snow
Against her own will
For the voices within
She dragged herself
And dug a hole
Grasping hands
Threw dirt down inside
Burying her with words alive
She hit the bottom, it was a muffled place
Emptied and tied into herself
A mess of glass and knots abound
The cold crept in
So she fell farther down
Her soul was fading
Hands still digging, looking for a way out
She found only more soil
The voices kept her knees locked
The hands, they threw more rocks
They weighed her down
She breathed in the Earth
Lost parts of herself
They sank away, rotted, and died
The voices were as razors

Cutting apart her mind
Until silently, surely
Her roots took hold
And she began to rise
A light came in the darkness
Through the dirt and stone
Cuts still came to her flesh as she grew
Yet the light's warmth seemed unattainable
So far out of reach
Still she grew in the suffocation
Her voices quieted and she began to miss
the noise
Felt all the more lonely
Slowly the light grew closer
A speck became a spark
The spark became the sun
She carried herself out of the mud
Scarred, dirty, cold, and shaking
But a smile on her face
And the voices in her head
Were telling her to live instead

There Will Be An Ending

No fire burns forever
This is something I should've known

But I couldn't see, except for the smoke
I don't know if I even believed

Anything that was set in front of me
Hindsight is always bathed in clarity

Someone had to tell me I was alive
Before my heart decided to restart

There's no fire that will burn forever
I'm opening up my eyes now

I'm feeling the raindrops kissing my flesh
Forcing me to inhale at the jolts

The deluge will come, the relief
Sometimes it helps me forget

Though it's deafening and silent all at once
Now I see through the mist

No fire burns forever
This is something I should've known

**The Way It's Always Been
(Is Not The Way Things Have To Be)**

It's time to stop relying on safety harnesses
and backup lines
I cut the cord because it's better in this
instance to meet the ground
As it rises to meet me at the beginning
of the end again
The wind screams secrets in my ears I don't
catch
It couldn't say anything to get me to look
back up
Because I can get through this
Step back into the picture frame and walk
around
In that precious, cruel moment forever
preserved
I would take her face in my hands and wipe
away her tears with soft thumbs
Press my forehead to hers and say,
"The failures are too many to count, but
I'm still here."
She woke up on the wrong side of reality
So my eyes meet hers and I tell her to get up

It's time to stop relying on help and looking
to the hills
I peer into the chasm before me and grip
her hand
We take a running leap into the deep end
The water whispers to try and guide me
further down
It couldn't offer anything to make me
pay attention
Because I have to get through this
I would race and run until I find her sitting
shivering in the snow
I would take her hands and squeeze her
tight to show her real warmth
Press my forehead to hers and say,
"The world is too big to carry,
but I'm still here."
She can't see the light at the end of the
tunnel
So my voice softens and I tell her to keep
trying

It's time to stop expecting others to
take action and offer their hands
I stare down the wall we've made and raise
the hammer over my shoulder

The bricks protest too much while they're
being laid to waste
They swear they don't serve the power
I think they do
I can't listen, I know now what I have to do
Because I can live through this
I go back into this memory of hers
decorated with ripped edges
and muffled voices
I would tap her shoulder and
she spins to meet me
Without a spark in her eyes
I would press my forehead to hers and say,
"I stopped waiting and I'm still here."
I don't think I can ignore this need
anymore
So I take my hands out of my pockets and
bend to her level
And I tell her I've always been here

Entanglements

Love was never an easy thing
Two lovers with one soul
Through all the ups and downs
We float upon this endless sea
Our lives intertwined
Small, shattered pieces of our matrices
Fused and repaired with gold
We stand, our power flowing
Despite the lashes and the throes
Biting our tongues through the diminution
Trapped far apart from one another
We will carry our worlds and
Baby, they'll get what they deserve
Baby, they'll reap what they sow
It almost feels as if nothing changes
You will understand someday despite
The beats seeming off and patterns
unfurled
Promise me
Whatever beasts may come
Whatever hell this heaven may bring
Anything that follows
Love from afar but stronger still
Human to the very last

The Eldest One

Somehow I am the eldest one
I'm not who I used to be before
I'm not who I wanted to be back then
I am simultaneously more and
less than I expected
If I told of where I'd been
No one would ever believe me
The more I try to remember
The more I realize I've forgotten

What am I supposed to create?
If I am not the one favored by fate?
Such was my life, so is my life
Because I am at the mercy of
nonrecreational chemicals
The bruises on my neck match a pattern
of fingertips
And venom veiled words
They catch on my canines
I promise I tried; I gave it my all

I collected my pieces and pride
Without knowing what came next
Without knowing what to believe in

My mistakes remained too heavy for
absolution
Part of me is lost in the unknown
But if I fought for it back, I'd be nowhere
again
I am the scars that never healed
Wounded by my own expectations

All of these movements are synchronized
beats
Each breath in and out while time passes
These pressure points I keep pushing back
They steal the blood from my veins
My universes and entropic, empathic
journeys
Still flashing, refusing to capsize
I was broken in my prime, but I embrace it

I hold force in my gaze to prove I can
Fluctuating between emotional and
emotionless
But at that time, I chose to let it flow,
this vicious vein
Though it short-circuits my mind
And twists knots into my spine
I'll become a beast if I'm pushed far enough

It's deep in my eyes
They ignored the darkness there
I can promise, I'll always be dangerous

Darkest December

Daddy are you out there somewhere?
Daddy isn't there anything you can say?
I must have called for you thousands of
times
Didn't you hear me?
I guess you're too far away
You're really far away
I'm not sure it's okay
But you're really so far now
I hate the irony of it and
I can't believe that they released
a new album after
And one of the tracks is for you
It hurts so much every time
I can't sleep
Worse than that other song which
tears me apart
You were my ringer, Daddy
Chaos is giving all the orders
I'm trying my best to do it right
But it feels so pointless and hopeless
I dropped all of my dreams
That I was clutching to my chest
And I can't keep up with the speed

at which they're falling away
Sinking like tarnished coins in the fountain
Empty wishes never to be fulfilled
That first birthday
Well
That wasn't even the worst one
I wish giving up would work sometimes
It was the second one
The fact you're still gone
I hate that
Someday
I hope I can fly next to you
Keep flying on, one minute you're gone
Next I know you'll be there
And the darkest December will be long past
All I can think about is you
It's all that I can do
Because it all hurts me

Autobiography

Baby
Daughter
Granddaughter
Only child
Vermonter
Toddler
Child
Older sister
Friend
Best friend
Child of divorce
Patient
Difficult child
Step-daughter
First grader
Second grader
Third grader
Soccer player
Fourth grader
Fifth grader
Middle schooler
Sprinter
Hurdler
Runner

High schooler
Patient
JV only
Cross country runner
Long distance runner
Second best
Pretty
Girlfriend
Ex-girlfriend
Writer
Photographer
Depressed
Anxious
Ugly
Suicide survivor
Prisoner
Should-have-cut-vertically
Woman
Cat mother
High school graduate
Lover
College student
Major-changer
Club president
Award winner
Scholarship recipient

Champion
Professional photographer
Published
Bachelor degree recipient
Graduate student
Strongwoman
Scientist
Masters degree recipient
Major depressive
Anxious
PhD student
New Yorker
Patient Visitor
Cancer researcher
Lab member
Dutiful daughter
Eulogist
Estate administrator
Daughter who lost her Dad

Acknowledgements

There are several people without whom this book would not have seen the light of day, much less eyes other than my own. I want to thank my brother, Sam, who has gone through all of this with me. I want to thank my significant other, Dexter Thomas for his support and time going over some of the works to give me first reactions. I also thank my friends Nicole Kulakowski and Florisela Herrejon Chavez for their help finding the right words. Finally, I must thank my friend Chaz Scala (who is also a poet, check her out @chaz.writes!) for encouraging me to put this together and answering questions I had about the process.

About the Author

Chiara Evans is a PhD in Pharmacology candidate at Weill Cornell and Memorial Sloan Kettering Cancer Center in New York City where she studies regulation of normal and malignant hematopoietic stem cells. Before this, she obtained Bachelor's and Master's degrees in Pharmaceutical Sciences in Albany, coming there from Vermont. When not in lab, she can be found writing, in the gym, or at home with her cat, Bane and significant other, Dexter.

Her public Instagram is: @darkest.december.